LOST PINES PUBLISHING

ASC 606 for Individual Contributors

Application of the FASB Standards for the "Doers" of Organizations

First published by Lost Pines Publishing 2024

Copyright © 2024 by Lost Pines Publishing

All rights reserved. No part of this publication may be reproduced, stored or transmitted in any form or by any means, electronic, mechanical, photocopying, recording, scanning, or otherwise without written permission from the publisher. It is illegal to copy this book, post it to a website, or distribute it by any other means without permission.

First edition

This book was professionally typeset on Reedsy.
Find out more at reedsy.com

"The best accountants are not just number-crunchers; they're financial storytellers"

JESSICA TURNER

Contents

Preface ii
1 Chapter 1: 2014-09, Revenue from Contracts with Customers... 1
2 Chapter 2: Identifying the Contract with the Customer 5
3 Chapter 3: Identifying The Performance Obligations of the... 11
4 Chapter 4: Determining The Transaction Price 15
5 Chapter 5: Allocate the Transaction Price to the Performance... 19
6 Chapter 6: Recognize Revenue When/As the Entity Satisfies... 23
7 Chapter 7: Identifying and Accounting for the Incremental... 28
8 Chapter 8: Changes to Disclosures and Reporting 33
Conclusion 38
Citations 39
Also by Lost Pines Publishing 42

Preface

In 2015, the Financial Accounting Standards Board introduced the Accounting Standards Update 2014-09, *Revenue from Contracts with Customers* (Topic 606). This new series of standards constituted a radical break from traditional accounting methods for recognizing revenue on contracts and other expenses. Its purpose was to normalize the recognition rules across various industries for improved reporting and comparison.

I was at a crossroads when I began my journey toward ASC 606 compliance within my organization. Do I need to go back to school? Will this affect my ability to perform within my organization? How do I wade through the mess of Google Ads for accounting software to answer my basic questions?

You are not alone if you're experiencing the painful shift from the formerly acceptable GAAP rules to ASC 606 standards. I've been an accountant in the software development industry for more than a decade. I have devoted my expertise to a small startup of fewer than 30 employees in the heart of the New Silicon Valley—Austin, Texas. The shift in software development from perpetual licenses with maintenance to SaaS subscriptions coincided with the change to ASC 606, driving clients' and companies' high demand for warm bodies in the accounting suite and runbooks that are affordable and easy to integrate into current internal documentation.

This short reference guide is intended for individual contributors in the accounting profession with an accounting background and a basic understanding of FASB ASC 606. It covers both day-to-day use cases and the methodologies that make FASB ASC 606 indispensable within organizations subject to routine auditing. This guide is not intended to replace sitting for the CPA exam, nor is it part of any qualified CPE. Its main scope is to quickly answer questions about ASC 606 and provide practical application examples.

Those with a firm grasp of the ASC 606 will become an asset to any accounting team, and you don't have to go back to school to help your team bring your business goals to life in a safe, controlled, and compliant environment. Welcome to *ASC 606 For Individual Contributors*.

1

Chapter 1: 2014-09, Revenue from Contracts with Customers (Topic 606)

"ASC 606 was a term my controllers and CFOs started throwing around in about 2018/ 2019, somewhere in there. I gleaned information in bits and pieces from meetings and I asked some questions. But I never got a firm grasp, and it didn't affect us much then. Our clients were still mostly selling software licenses with maintenance contracts (with and without hardware) that they downloaded on their machines, and they were not yet hosting a viable SaaS alternative. But I was unprepared as I got into 2023, and my pre-revenue SaaS client got their very first contract. I woefully underestimated ASC 606,"

Accounting Standards Update 2014-09, Revenue from Contracts with Customers will be affectionately referred to as ASC 606. The first step to applying the new guidance is to understand it. Why did the standards need to change (who told FASB there was a problem)? How will organizations benefit from the shift in guidance? What challenges will an organization face while switching from previously accepted GAAP and IFRS rules to the new standards? Once the context and framework are understood, applying the standards will naturally make more sense.

Well, why did FASB decide that it needed new standards? Financial statement users strongly desired more standardized rules for recognizing revenue. They suggested to the Board that it would be useful for companies to be more open with how and when they recognize revenue, especially since this concept is the most widely used basis for an organization's performance. Previously, organizations reported on their accounting practices and relayed how revenue recognition fit into their business. The problem is that financial statement users (investors, shareholders, banks, etc.) needed help comparing public and private companies within a given industry, never mind comparing companies from different industries.

Who is "they"? Financial statement users consist of committees and councils whose role is to advise the Board. There are several. The FASB Advisory Group; The Financial Accounting Standards Advisory Council; the Private Company Council; the Emerging Issues Task Force; the Investor Advisory Committee; the Not-For-Profit Advisory Committee and the Small Business Advisory Committee. More information about these groups and their role in the process of creating new codifications, or amending old ones, can be found on the FASB website at https://www.fasb.org/about-us/advisory-groups

The key objectives the Board set out to accomplish can be summarized by: Improve deficiencies and weaknesses in the existing guidance and provide authoritative guidance where there previously was none. Simply put, if there is minimal guidance or none on a particular revenue matter, ASC 606 is to be applied. However, if there is guidance and a framework already existing, then the existing standards should be applied first, then ASC 606. The Board sought to normalize GAAP and IFRS revenue recognition rules and practices. Their goal is, and has been for a long time, to align the two frameworks as much as possible. The Board also wanted to simplify the accounting process and the preparation of financial statements. This simplification helps improve the comparability of revenue recognition practices across public, private, and not-for-profit organizations. The new standard is beneficial for medium and large organizations that are not publicly traded. Previously, SOX Compliance was the only framework for these larger organizations, even though it was optional and not always relevant.

For Individual contributors, the accounting guidelines change from industry-specific and transaction-specific rules to more standardized rules that can be applied universally. You could take the accounting experience you gained at your software company to your new place of employment, no matter what industry that may be in. The benefit to organizations is a more simplified and concise way of interpreting financial statements. The most significant improvement is a more specific view of the profitability of a contract.

These changes and benefits do not come without a bit of pain. ASC 606 requires more, *much more*, disclosures and explanations about revenue recognition. This extra work will become evident during the audit process for companies that must be audited or reviewed by a bank. The switch from previous accounting standards to ASC 606 might require rigorous changes to subledgers and accounting estimates, require an organization to maintain more documentation, and potentially have broader implications for the business. Standard Policies and Procedures should also be updated for the accounting or operations teams. This work can be very time-consuming, on top of an already packed schedule that can't stop. Payroll stops for no one and nothing. Some individual contributors may have an increased workload as their organization switches to the new standard. The new standards also require changes to how organizations present the costs of acquiring revenue-generating contracts. This new presentation will require changes to account groupings and position on the balance sheet.

What do these new standards specifically apply to? Revenue from Contracts with Customers. Of course, there have always been organizations whose income is based on contracts—construction companies, Law Firms, Professional Service Providers, etc. Software Development is one of the industries that has experienced the most technological change over the past 10 years. Software development changed from selling a good to selling a service, creating huge pitfalls in the existing guidance quickly. What revenue was once recognized when the software was sold, now has to be evaluated about the type of control transferred, payment terms, and performance obligations.

Now that there is plenty of context for the new standard, what is ASC 606? ASC 606 presents a framework based on 5 principles:

1. Identifying the Contract with Customer
2. Identify the Performance Obligations of the Contract
3. Determine Transaction Price
4. Allocate the Transaction Price to the Performance Obligations In the Contract
5. Recognize Revenue When or As the Entity Satisfies the Performance Obligations in the Contract

The following chapters will examine each principle in more depth and provide examples of how to apply these standards. They will also highlight some key terms Individual Contributors might hear in the accounting industry, from implementation to everyday discussion of ASC 606.

2

Chapter 2: Identifying the Contract with the Customer

"Contracts were never something we focused much on in our accounting classes. I took one class in 2014 about business law, and it was dry, hard to understand, and somewhat vague in its context. The textbook didn't do a great job of relating the topics of contracts to accounting principles. At work, no one ever said anything to me about a contract until they reviewed an invoice and found an error. Then the question was, "Well, did you read the contract?". I never had access to the contract, let alone a working knowledge or understanding. Understanding contracts was one of the biggest learning curves in my shift from creating an invoice for a license, to invoicing Software as a Service. My role also went from just making sure we got paid, to enforcing the contract; and that requires a bit more backbone and thick skin,".

Identifying a contract with a customer is the first, and one of the most critical, steps in revenue recognition under ASC 606. A contract with a customer is defined as an agreement between two or more parties that creates enforceable rights and obligations. According to ASC 606, a contract exists if the following criteria are met:

- Approval and Commitment: The parties involved must approve the contract (in writing, orally, or by other customary business practices) and be committed to fulfilling their obligations.
- Identifiable Rights: The rights regarding goods or services to be transferred must be identifiable for each party.
- Payment Terms: The payment terms for the goods or services to be transferred must be identifiable.
- Commercial Substance: The contract must have commercial substance, meaning the risk, timing, or amount of the entity's future cash flows is expected to change because of the contract.
- Collectability: It must be probable that the entity or organization will collect the consideration (payment) to which it will be entitled in exchange for the goods or services that will be transferred to the customer.

While the criteria above are used for identifying a contract, what follows are the steps to see if the above criteria exist.

1. Review Agreements: Analyze all agreements with the customer to determine if they meet the criteria. Items to review include written contracts, oral agreements, and customary business practices. For an individual contributor, this is completed by a combination of other individuals in the business; like a Sales Account Executive and their management, the Controller, or General Counsel (if the organization has it, if not, they'll likely engage outside counsel) and the CFO or CEO. Usually, by the time it is ready to be actioned by a "doer" in operations or accounting, the agreement is already fully executed (fully signed and dated by both parties).
2. Assess Customer's Ability and Intention: Evaluate the customer's creditworthiness and the intention to pay. Collectability is assessed based on the customer's ability and intention to pay the promised

CHAPTER 2: IDENTIFYING THE CONTRACT WITH THE CUSTOMER

consideration when it is due. *"Many organizations require their customer's Dun & Bradstreet Identification Number, or DUNS number. D&B is a business credit reporting agency, like Experian or Equifax for individuals. This rating can help in determining if a customer can receive payment terms. Just like individual credit, if customers always pay their vendors late, their credit rating will decrease. If their credit is low, terms of the agreement may mean the customer has to pay the day they receive their invoice, instead of being able to pay 30 or 60 days after the effective date of the contract or invoice,"*

3. Identify Contract Modifications: If the contract has any modifications, determine whether they should be treated as a separate contract or as part of the existing contract. A contract modification exists if the parties agree to a change in the contract's scope or price (or both).

4. Evaluate Combination of Contracts: Determine if two or more contracts should be combined, and accounted for, as a single contract. This is necessary if the contracts are negotiated as a package with a single commercial objective, or if the amount of consideration to be paid in one contract depends on the price or performance of the other contract, then the goods or services promised in the contracts represent a single performance obligation.

"Individual contributors often fall into a trap when it comes to identifying when it is okay to take action on a contract. In the past, the contract was signed by someone in an organization that did not have the authority to do so. Only certain people, C-Suite Officers usually, or Chief Counsel, have the authority to create liabilities and acquire assets for an organization. If an Individual Contributor is unsure of their authority in their organization, they need to find out. Usually, it's quite limited. As ICs, the ability to proceed with invoicing and recognizing revenue on a contract requires approval and should

be documented in a Standard Operating Procedure. The internal control for this process is either automated approval workflows in an ERP or oversight by a manager,"

Example 1: Written Contract – *Software the Old-Fashioned Way*

A software company signs a written contract with a customer to deliver a software license and provide technical support for one year. The contract clearly states the deliverables, payment terms, and is signed by both parties.

- **Approval and Commitment**: The contract is signed by people in the organizations with the authority to do so.
- **Identifiable Rights**: The software license, support services, and delivery are clearly defined.
- **Payment Terms**: Specified in the contract.
- **Commercial Substance**: The company's cash flows will change due to the contract.
- **Collectability**: The customer has a good credit rating, and payment is probable per the payment terms.

This contract meets all criteria and is identified as a contract with a customer.

Example 2: Written Contract – *Software as a Service/Subscription*

- **Approval and Commitment**: The contract is signed by people in the organizations with the authority to do so.
- **Identifiable Rights**: The software access, authorized users, and implementation steps/milestones are clearly defined, as well as any support services that might be included in the subscription (updates, upgrades, support tickets, etc)
- **Payment Terms**: Specified in the contract.
- **Commercial Substance**: The company's cash flows will change

due to the contract.
- **Collectability**: The customer has a good credit rating, and payment is probable per the payment terms.

This contract meets all criteria and is identified as a contract with a customer.

Example 3: Oral Agreement
A freelance graphic designer agrees over the phone to create a logo for a local business. The terms of payment and the deliverables are discussed, but nothing is written down.

- **Approval and Commitment**: The parties have agreed verbally.
- **Identifiable Rights**: The service to be provided (logo creation) is clear.
- **Payment Terms**: Discussed but not documented.
- **Commercial Substance**: The designer's cash flows will change due to the agreement.
- **Collectability**: The local business has a history of paying freelancers on time.

This contract meets all criteria and is identified as a contract with a customer.

If the oral agreement aligns with customary business practices in this context and all criteria are met, this can be identified as a contract with a customer.

Identifying a contract with a customer requires careful evaluation of the agreement against specific criteria. Ensuring that all criteria are met is essential for proper revenue recognition. This involves a detailed review of the agreement's terms, the parties' rights and obligations, and the commercial substance and collectability of the consideration (payment).

3

Chapter 3: Identifying The Performance Obligations of the Contract

"*Of course, I knew what an item was, and the risk and rewards transferred allowed us to recognize revenue. We learned that in school...12 years ago. We prove that the customer received their license key, and the revenue was eligible for recognition. What changed was this concept of transfer of control rather than transfer of the benefits of the item. Contracts with customers exist almost in a parallel universe. On one plane, the control of the asset transfers to the customer. On the other plane, the actual handoff of the goods or the software implementation. These things sometimes happen simultaneously; other times, it's not so obvious or takes much longer. SaaS is exactly that way. The transfer of control is on the day the contract is fully executed even though the customer has never even logged in. It took me a long time to understand this. I would tell my manager, "We can't invoice this yet, the cloud team hasn't provisioned the licenses." And he would say, "Yeah, but the contract has been signed." I was baffled, but I went with it and accepted that is how things are now. But the reason was never fully explained, and I didn't know there was a question to be asked. My advice to all Individual Contributors is always to ask, "But...why?".*"

Identifying performance obligations in a contract is the next step in revenue recognition for ASC 606. A performance obligation is a promise to transfer to a customer either 1) a good or a service (or a bundle of goods or services) that is distinct, or 2) the transfer of a series of distinct goods or services that are substantially the same and have the same pattern of transfer to the customer. Performance obligations are always assessed at the time of the contract inception (commencement or beginning).

The two features of performance obligations that must be highlighted are the transfer of control of an asset and the asset itself (goods and/or services). Transfer refers to a change in control. Goods and services are an asset. Control of an asset is transferred when the customer gains the ability to direct the use of the asset and obtains substantially all the remaining economic benefits of the asset. The customer's acceptance of the assets plays an essential role in the transfer of control. The timing of the transfer of control for revenue recognition will be covered at length in Chapter 6: Recognizing Revenue When/As the Entity Satisfies the Performance Obligations

There are two main criteria for determining whether or not a good or service (or a bundle of goods or services) is distinct. Both criteria must be met for a good or service to be distinct. Goods can be explicit (stated in the contract), or implicit (arising from established business practices).

- Capability: The customer can benefit from the goods or services either on their own or together with other readily available resources. That is, is the good or service capable of being used with what the customer already has purchased, either from this entity or another third party?
- Distinct within the context of the contract: This assessment focuses on whether the nature of the entity's promise is to transfer each good or service individually or to transfer a combined item that is

greater than the sum of its parts.

An example of a distinct good is a software license that the customer can use independently. Or a training session provided as part of a software implementation contract that can be conducted independently. However, if a software license requires significant customization or integration services to be functional (aka a single deliverable), then it is not a distinct good. If goods or services are not distinct individually, they need to be combined with other promised goods or services until you identify a bundle that is distinct.

Example 1: Software License with Customization Services

- **Promises:** Software license, customization services, and post-contract customer support (PCS).
- **Assessment -**
- Software license and customization are not distinct because the customer cannot benefit from the software without customization.
- PCS is distinct because it can be provided separately from the software and customization.

Example 2: Construction Contract

- **Promises:** Design, construction, and maintenance.
- **Assessment -**
- Design and construction are typically not distinct because they form a combined output.
- Maintenance is distinct as it occurs after construction and provides separate benefits.

Identifying performance obligations requires thoroughly analyzing the contract and the nature of the promised goods or services. Document the judgment applied in identifying performance obligations, especially in complex contracts. Consider the economic factors, customer expectations, and contract nuances in identifying performance obligations. If a customer has the option to purchase additional goods or services at a discount, this might create a performance obligation. Determine if warranties provide assurance (not a separate performance obligation) or a service (distinct performance obligation).

4

Chapter 4: Determining The Transaction Price

"Transaction prices are somewhat ambiguous to an individual contributor. Usually, a business has a whole department of people who work together with the finance team to determine what price each item (or bundle of items) should be sold for. They determine who is eligible for a discount, and how much of a discount can be given before it's not profitable. At one of my clients, the transaction price is clearly laid out in plain language and bold print. At other clients, it is not so easy to glean this information from 11 pages of legalese. It requires careful examination of the contract, and I always ask if there is ever any doubt. I would rather an Account Executive talk down to me for not understanding the contract than make a guess, get it wrong, and then have to fix it. Or worse, have to explain it. More clarification is required when working on smaller clients whose invoicing process consists of just one person without the control of management oversight."

Determining the transaction price involves calculating the total amount to be paid by the buyer to the seller for goods or services provided. Several factors, such as discounts, rebates, the type of considerations, and any other adjustments can influence the transaction price. Several different kinds of considerations, or payments, can be included in a contract with a customer

- Fixed Consideration: Identify the fixed portion of the transaction price (the most common type of consideration).
- Variable Consideration: Estimate variable consideration using the expected value or the most likely amount method. Keep estimates of variable consideration to the amount that will most likely not result in a significant reversal of revenue when the uncertainty is resolved.
- Significant Financing Component: Consider the time value of money if the timing of payments provides a substantial benefit of financing to either the customer or the entity. Adjust the transaction price for the effects of the financing component, if significant.
- Non-Cash Consideration: Measure non-cash consideration at fair value. If fair value cannot be reasonably estimated, reference the stand-alone selling price of the goods or services promised in exchange for the consideration.
- Consideration Payable to a Customer: Account for any consideration payable to the customer as a reduction of the transaction price unless the payment is in exchange for a distinct good or service that the customer transfers to the entity.

Here are the general steps to determine the transaction price:

1. Identify the Base Price: This is the initial price of the goods or services before any adjustments. Base price is also commonly referred to as list price
2. Adjust for Discounts: Subtract any trade, volume, or early payment discounts.

CHAPTER 4: DETERMINING THE TRANSACTION PRICE

3. **Adjust for Rebates and Credits:** Subtract any rebates or credits that apply.
4. **Include Additional Charges:** Add any additional charges, such as shipping fees, handling fees, or other surcharges.
5. **Consider Variable Considerations:** Estimate and include any variable considerations, such as performance bonuses, penalties, or contingent payments. This step may involve probability-weighted estimates or other statistical methods to account for uncertainties.
6. **Adjust for Payment Terms:** Consider the effect of payment terms, such as extended payment plans, which might require adjusting the price for the time value of money.
7. **Review for Non-Cash Considerations:** If the transaction includes non-cash considerations, such as the transfer of non-monetary assets, determine their fair value and include them in the transaction price.

All of this can sound a little daunting. It can be summed up for "doers" as the first real step of establishing revenue. The invoice. Identifying performance obligations, transfer of control, and transaction prices are all just lines on an invoice. Essentially, how much is an entity going to charge the customer? Are there any special conditions that might require extra attention or additional questions? ICs are very rarely left to evaluate types of consideration on their own, and most only deal with Fixed Considerations that might have some discounts.

Example Scenario

Let's consider an example where a company, XYZ Corp, enters into a contract to sell 100 units of a product to a customer for $10,000. The contract also includes a potential performance bonus of $1,000 if the units are delivered within a specified time frame.

1. **Contract Identification:**

- XYZ Corp and the customer have signed a contract agreeing to the terms and conditions.

1. **Performance Obligations:**

- The performance obligation is the delivery of 100 units of the product.

1. **Transaction Price Determination:**

- Fixed consideration: $10,000.
- Variable consideration: Estimate the likelihood of earning the $1,000 performance bonus.
- XYZ Corp estimates that there is an 80% chance of earning the bonus. Using the expected value method: $1,000 * 80% = $800.
- Total transaction price: $10,000 + $800 = $10,800..

Determining the transaction price involves careful consideration of all terms and conditions in the contract, including any variable elements and the time value of money (significant financing). By following the outlined steps, entities can ensure that they accurately determine and allocate the transaction price in accordance with accounting standards.

5

Chapter 5: Allocate the Transaction Price to the Performance Obligation

"When I was in school, terms that were used to describe the price of an item or service was Fair Market Value, or Replacement Value. VSOE was a term that I learned on the job, and because my role as an individual contributor was limited to just processing invoices for items, I did not need to know what it was. My role has changed significantly with time and technology. I'm still an individual contributor, and my mindset has stayed back in the classroom. I had to venture out of what was comfortable, back out into that parallel universe where the transaction price is what we send the customer on an invoice, and the SSP was what we were going to use to establish the ratios for allocating the transaction price and recognizing revenue,".

The transaction price (the price on the invoice we send to the customer) is allocated proportionately to each performance obligation based on the SSP. The SSP is the price at which an entity would sell a promised good or service separately to a customer.

A significant shift in determining a revenue allocation under ASC 606 for Software companies is from the VSOE (ASC 605), Vendor Specific

Objective Evidence, method to SSP, Stand-alone Selling Price. VSOE was the allocation standard at the beginning of the rise of the Software Subscription and was based on stringent historical data to support the stand-alone selling price. Moving away from VSO to SSP allows more distinct performance obligations under a contract as they could now be distinct without previously establishing VSOE. Under ASC 606, the flexibility in determining SSP allows companies to better align revenue recognition with the economics of their transactions, potentially leading to more accurate financial reporting.

Any changes in the transaction price (e.g., a price increase or decrease depending on the contract terms at the start of the renewal period) should be allocated to the performance obligations on the same basis as at contract inception.

Organizations can use several methods to estimate SSP

- Observable Prices: this is the price at which the company sells a good or service on a stand-alone basis with regularity to similar customers under similar circumstances. The transaction price in this case is the SSP.
- Adjusted Market Assessment Approach: this approach evaluates the market in which goods and services are sold and estimates the price that customers in that market would be willing to pay
- Expected Cost Plus Margin Approach: This approach estimates the costs of providing the goods or services and adds an appropriate margin
- Residual Approach: This approach is used when the SSP is highly variable or uncertain. It allocates the remainder of the transaction price to the good or service by subtracting the SSPs of the other goods or services in the contract

Challenges often arise when trying to determine SSP. It can be complex,

CHAPTER 5: ALLOCATE THE TRANSACTION PRICE TO THE PERFORMANCE...

especially when there is no observable price. Changes in market fluctuations can affect the SSP over time. Bundled pricing (*"I don't know about you, but bundled pricing is my least favorite type of pricing,".*) presents challenges in allocating discounts or promotional prices across multiple products or services. If a discount is provided on the bundle, allocate the discount proportionately based on the standalone selling prices unless it is obvious that the discount relates to a specific performance obligation. If the transaction price includes variable consideration, estimate the amount using the expected value or the most likely amount method. Companies transitioning from the old ASC 605 to ASC 606 had to adapt from using VSOE to determining SSP, often requiring internal processes and systems changes to estimate standalone selling prices.

Example:

Imagine you have a contract to deliver software and ongoing support. The standalone selling price for the software is $8,000 and for the support is $2,000. The total transaction price is $9,000 (Remember, the transaction price is net of all adjustments to the base price in Chapter 4). Here's how you allocate it:

1. **Calculate the total standalone selling price:**

Total Standalone Selling Price = 8,000+2,000 =10,000

1. **Calculate the proportion of each component:**

Proportion for Software = 8,000 / 10,000 = 80%
Proportion for Support = 2,000 / 10,000 = 20%

1. **Allocate the transaction price:**

Allocated Price for Software = 9,000 × 80% = 7,200

Allocated Price for Support = 9,000 × 20% = 1,800

Allocating the transaction price to performance obligations guarantees that revenue is recognized in a manner that matches the transfer of goods or services to customers. By following the steps outlined above, you can systematically allocate the transaction price to performance obligations and recognize revenue appropriately.

6

Chapter 6: Recognize Revenue When/As the Entity Satisfies the Performance Obligations

"As an elder millennial, a scene from SpongeBob SquarePants always flutters into my mind when I think about the principles of ASC 606. It's the episode about the Krusty Krab Training Video, where SpongeBob has to learn all of these key principles about his workplace before he can learn to make a Krabby Patty. And now we come to it! Our Krabby Patty: Recognizing Revenue! There are a lot of tools out there to assist in the recognition process. Everything from formulas in Excel to modules in a large ERP, to bolt-on software for QuickBooks Online. There is an option for every sized organization. And I've got experience with a lot of them. Of course, my favorite is revenue recognition templates in Sage Intacct. They just make it so easy. But you still have to be able to effectively tell the template what to do with the line in an invoice. Different items can be recognized over different periods, and you have to know which template to choose. It's important to adapt to your organization's changing landscape and the types of contracts they make with customers. Some items are recognized over the life of the contract and have a template of the straight-line variety. Others are recognized on a percentage of completion, and others are accelerated. And all three can occur on the same invoice,".

Revenue is recognized when control of the promised good or service is transferred to the customer. The amount of revenue recognized should reflect the consideration to which the entity expects to be entitled in exchange for those goods or services. The idea of transferring control first appeared in Chapter 3 when the contract's performance obligations were identified. Again, control of an asset is the ability to direct the use of, and obtain substantially all of the remaining economic benefits of, an asset. Transferring control can happen at a point in time or over time. At what point control is transferred is determined at the inception of the contract.

Generally, revenue recognition under accounting standard ASC 606 emphasizes the transfer of control as the critical factor. This is a change from previous standards, where control was transferred when the customer assumed all of the asset's risks and rewards. Transfer of control determines when revenue should be recognized, focusing on the customer's ability to direct the use of the asset or service. Risks and rewards, on the other hand, focus on legal ownership and financial implications.

When control is transferred over time, one of the following criteria has to be met:

- The customer simultaneously receives and consumes the benefits provided by the entity's performance as the entity performs it
- **Example - Subscription Services**: Revenue for subscription services (e.g., software as a service) is recognized over time because the customer receives and consumes the benefits as the service is provided.
- The entity's performance creates or enhances an asset that the customer controls as the asset is created or enhanced
- **Example: Construction Contracts**: Revenue is typically recognized over time for long-term construction contracts using an input

method such as the cost-to-cost method, which measures progress based on costs incurred relative to total expected costs.
- The asset has no alternative use to the entity and has an enforceable right to payment for performance completed to date

When the criteria for control to be transferred over time is not met, then the control is transferred at a point in time. The criteria for transfer to be at a point in time are more reminiscent of previous standards and include, but are not limited to:

- The entity has a present right to payment for the asset
- The customer has legal title to the asset. Legal title means the owner has the right to transfer ownership to another party, and it is recognized by law. The legal title often includes responsibilities such as paying property taxes and complying with regulations
- The entity has transferred physical possession of the asset
- **Example - Product Sales**: Revenue for product sales is usually recognized at a point in time when control of the product transfers to the customer, which is often at the time of delivery.
- The customer has the significant risks and rewards of ownership of the asset
- The customer has accepted the asset. Acceptance by the customer is an essential feature of a contract. Once the customer has accepted the goods as fulfilled by specifications in the contract, the customer cannot later reject the goods, they have to pay for them per the contract terms

When recognizing revenue over time, an entity must measure its progress toward complete satisfaction of the performance obligation. Methods for measuring progress include:

- **Output Methods**: Recognize revenue based on direct measurements of the value transferred to the customer (e.g., surveys of performance completed to date, appraisals of results achieved). An example of the output method would be the purchase of Software.
- **Input Methods**: Recognize revenue based on the entity's efforts or inputs to satisfy a performance obligation (e.g., costs incurred, resources consumed, labor hours expended). A rather obvious example of input methods is the performance of professional services. Care should be taken not to overstate revenue in this method.

The entity should measure its progress toward completion using the method that best depicts its performance and the transfer of control of goods and services.

These concepts outline what an individual contributor does when making journal entries to recognize revenue. Once the amount of revenue assigned to each performance obligation is identified and the timing of the control transfer is established, the actual journal entries can commence. Not all ERPs and software can accommodate all of the different revenue recognition scenarios, but they can do most of them. For a SaaS company where products are usually sold with an obvious stand-alone price, each product sold can be assigned a line and a revenue recognition template.

Sage Intacct is great for Software Licenses, Maintenance Contracts, Term Subscriptions (hosted on the customer's premises), SaaS Subscriptions (hosted on the entity's premises), Professional Services, and Post Contract Support. Each good or service is assigned its respective deferred revenue account (if different product lines must be broken out into separate deferred revenue and revenue accounts on their respective financial statements). Each revenue recognition schedule assigned to a template that posts over a given period, or at a point of time in the future,

CHAPTER 6: RECOGNIZE REVENUE WHEN/AS THE ENTITY SATISFIES...

creates the required Journal Entries to recognize revenue. Revenue is usually recognized immediately in the case of perpetual (owned forever) licenses and term licenses that are downloadable, but expire at the end of the contract term.

The principle of recognizing revenue when or as the entity satisfies performance obligations guarantees that revenue is recognized in a way that reflects the transfer of control of goods or services to customers. This approach provides more useful information to users of financial statements by aligning revenue recognition with the economic realities of business transactions.

7

Chapter 7: Identifying and Accounting for the Incremental Costs of Obtaining a Contract with a Customer

"The matching principle. The concept of matching expenses incurred to the revenue they create is nothing new. The matching principle is at the core of accrual accounting and is very important. Unlike revenue, this cannot be overstated (hahaha! I'm sorry, please don't block me). ASC 606 expands on this. As an Individual Contributor, it was never really explained to me when this change was made at my larger client's organization. Again, my little pre-revenue client provided the learning opportunity. Although, I guess now they aren't pre-revenue anymore. As it should have, their first contract with a customer resulted in sales commissions for the AE (Account Executive) that closed the deal. It was a three-year contract that would be billed annually, and his commission schedule was structured so that he would be paid a large portion at the inception of the contract, and then the remainder split over the next two years. My CFO created a prepaid commission subledger, and a prepaid commission account on the balance sheet grouped with our prepaid expenses. This seemed to get us most of the way there. We capitalized it and were amortizing it over the

CHAPTER 7: IDENTIFYING AND ACCOUNTING FOR THE INCREMENTAL...

contract's life. But there were pieces still missing. We were still operating as though the capital asset was tied to when the commission was paid, which is not in the spirit of accrual accounting or ASC 606. We owed him a large amount, but we were only recording the expense one month at a time in Sales Commissions Liability and Expense, and we were only establishing the asset when we paid the commission. But we owed him the whole amount due at signing per his contract! I talked myself in circles about this because I couldn't wrap my head around the process. And the reason for that was because my CFO was trying to avoid grossing up the balance sheet. But! It was also written in the comp plans that commission payment to the AE would be at the time the customer paid their invoice. I felt that we needed to accrue the entire commission because we owed it, and it was material. We go back into the parallel universe, where his commission expense is being amortized evenly over the three-year contract, but we're paying it on a different cadence. It just seemed that we were doing three things at once. Trying not to gross up the balance sheet, trying to accurately convey what we owed the AE, and balancing the accounting with protecting the business from cashflow shortfalls should the customer pay late. I convinced her to let me establish a Capitalized Commission Asset and accrue the entire liability. We're still tweaking it while we're waiting for our audit firm to review our method,".

The Matching Principle is at the core of ASC 606, not to mention accrual accounting in general. The matching principle is an accounting concept that requires that expenses be recorded in the same period as the revenues they generate. This principle aims to ensure that financial statements accurately reflect the company's performance during a specific period. The entire premise of accrual accounting hinges on a company not reflecting its costs as they are paid, but rather in the period they are incurred. Before ASC 606, most entities were recording expenses when they were incurred, and if that period was future, it was coded to prepaid, and if it was past, it was an accrued expense. Under

ASC 606, costs specifically for obtaining a contract, whether below the line or above the line, must be capitalized and amortized over the contract's life. This narrows the focus of the accrual from just overtime kind of getting close to the revenue period to an absolute period in time with its associated revenue.

The costs of acquiring a contract can be defined as the cost an entity incurs to obtain a contract with a customer that it would not ordinarily have incurred if the entity had not obtained the contract. In other words, the cost must be incremental. If the cost is incremental, it must be capitalized as an asset. The costs must also be evaluated for recoverability. If the costs are incremental and recoverable by the entity, they should be capitalized as an asset and amortized systematically in the same manner as the transfer of control over the related goods and services; in other words, in the same manner, revenue is recognized

The Board does give some respite to this requirement. Costs associated with contracts that are less than one year can be expensed in the period they are incurred. This is because revenue from contracts for less than one year can also be recognized in the period it is incurred. For example, a 6-month POC and its associated costs can be recognized at a point (usually when the contract is effective) rather than amortized over just 6 months. This might change if the POC results in the signing of a contract.

The most common example of incremental costs is sales commissions, but can also include direct labor, direct materials, contract management and supervision, insurance, deprecation of tools and equipment, payments to subcontractors, selling and marketing costs, bid and proposal costs, legal fees (only if the lawyer or firm agrees that fees would not be payable until after the completion of the contract negotiations) and travel costs (as long as they are explicitly chargeable to the customer in the contract).

Sales commissions, again, are incremental because it would not be a

CHAPTER 7: IDENTIFYING AND ACCOUNTING FOR THE INCREMENTAL...

cost the entity would pay had it not obtained the contract. Commissions are also considered recoverable because the cost can be expected to be recovered through future revenue from the contract. The percentage of commission the Account Executive receives is usually laid out in their sales compensation plan that is evaluated as part of their employment compensation package every year to ensure it aligns with current business practices. Once the contract details are determined, the Account Executive can be paid based on the terms of their contract, and those contracts usually contain language on the payment cadence (off-cycle payroll, or with the next upcoming payroll, net 45 days from the day the contract is signed, etc.) per the company's payroll policies. The expense and the revenue can then be recognized over the terms of the contract.

Example:

- An Account Executive obtains an Enterprise SaaS contract of $1,000,000 with a contract term of three years effective the day the last party signs the agreement, that date being June 1, 2024. The Entity has a policy of paying sales commissions on the next upcoming payroll
- The Account Executive's Sales Compensation Agreement states that they will receive 15% of the total contract as a commission. $1,000,000 X 15% = $150,000
- The commission is to be paid on the following schedule
- 80% of total commission to be paid at contract inception
- 10% of total commission to be paid at the beginning of year 2 of the contract
- 10% of total commission to be paid at the beginning of year 3 of the contract
- An accrual must be established for the total amount of the commission due. This is done by Debiting the Capitalized Cost of Acquiring

Contracts Account and Crediting Sales Commission Liability.
- The period over which the SaaS Revenue can be recognized is immediately after the last party signs the contract. Therefore, the amortization of the capitalized sales commissions must start at the same time. One month of commission expense will be recognized along with one month of revenue, in this case, a whole month because the contract was signed by the last party on June 1st.
- Sales commission liability will be relieved as the commission is paid. The payment for sales commissions occurs on the account executive's next paycheck, so the payroll entry will include a relief to the accrued sales commissions for 80% of the total commissions owed.
- In years 2 and 3, the accrual will be further relieved by the sales commission payment on the closest payroll around June 1st of the respective year.

Recognizing expenses to obtain a contract over the term of a contract involves allocating the costs associated with fulfilling a contract to the periods in which the related revenues are earned. This matching principle ensures that expenses are recognized in the same period as the revenues they help generate, providing a more accurate picture of financial performance.

Chapter 8: Changes to Disclosures and Reporting

"Here is another nitty, gritty reality check I received last year. Audits. For most of my time spent on enterprise software companies, they were privately owned by one or two investors and weren't required to be officially audited. The bank reviewed them as part of their debt covenants, but nothing too heavy in terms of work. One of our clients, a large one (over 100 employees) was acquired by a Venture Capital firm. They required audited financial statements. We had been tracking VSOE about a year prior, and they were switching to ASC 606 rather slowly, especially as they were finally launching their SaaS platform intending to eventually retire their other, non-SaaS, products (what developers call "end of life"). We were now not only changing accounting practices but also experiencing the burden of an audit where ASC 606 was required. I have never pulled so much documentation before. We learned about AR confirmations in school, and the only takeaway from that was that it wasn't required for any entity to respond. Well, when no one responds to your confirmation request (and those who do are alarmed because they don't understand the ask), that means pulling more documentation. I was kind of mean about it too. I stopped labeling files after about hour 12 or 13. I made them work for it. Not very *professional, but I was beaten down and still had to do my everyday job. My CFO and Controller at one client have spent whole days in conference rooms working on the narratives required for disclosures. I am so glad I don't do public accounting or audit work, though I'm told I would be good at it.,"*

ASC 606 requires entities to provide comprehensive disclosures that give financial statement users information about the nature, amount, timing, and uncertainty of revenue and cash flows arising from contracts with customers. Entities must disclose qualitative and quantitative information about their contracts with customers, the significant judgments and changes in judgments made in applying the guidance, and assets recognized from the costs to obtain or fulfill a contract.

The audit process has become more daunting for an individual contributor, with more samples, more confirmations, and more narratives. They require more proof that there was a valid contract, and that past valid contracts were paid. There are changes in how certain costs are presented on the balance sheet both for assets and liabilities. Along that vein, there are additional reporting requirements for changing aspects of a contract, like a customer's credit risk or changes in transaction price. The changes to disclosures mean adding new accounts, new subledgers or working files, and new tasks to the financial closing process. This can add hours to an already busy work schedule. Payroll, Collections, AP, Credit Card Reconciliations, etc. still have to go on during an audit. An IC should make sure they prioritize work so that everything gets done promptly without sacrificing quality…and sleep, which might happen from time to time.

One change from the previous standards is the process of disaggregation of revenue. Revenue should be disaggregated (broken out) into categories that depict how the nature, amount, timing, and uncertainty of revenue and cash flows are affected by economic factors. Categories may include:

CHAPTER 8: CHANGES TO DISCLOSURES AND REPORTING

- Type of good or service (e.g., major product lines)
- Geographical region
- Market or type of customer (e.g., government vs. non-government customers)
- Contract duration (short-term vs. long-term)
- Timing of revenue recognition (e.g., goods transferred at a point in time vs. services transferred over time)
- Sales channels (e.g., direct vs. indirect)

Another change from the previous standard is that Entities must disclose the opening and closing balances of receivables, contract assets, and contract liabilities. Additionally, they should provide:

- Revenue recognized in the reporting period that was included in the contract liability balance at the beginning of the period.
- Revenue recognized in the reporting period from performance obligations satisfied (or partially satisfied) in previous periods (e.g., changes in transaction price).

Disclosures must include information about performance obligations in contracts with customers, including:

- When the entity typically satisfies its performance obligations (e.g., upon shipment, upon delivery, as services are rendered).
- Significant payment terms (e.g., when payment is typically due, whether the contract has a significant financing component, or variable consideration amount).
- Nature of the goods or services that the entity has promised to transfer, highlighting any performance obligations to arrange for another party to transfer goods or services.
- Obligations for returns, refunds, and other similar obligations.

Entities must disclose the aggregate amount of the transaction price allocated to performance obligations that are unsatisfied (or partially unsatisfied) as of the end of the reporting period and an explanation of when they expect to recognize that amount as revenue. This can be presented in one of two ways:

- On a quantitative basis using time bands that are most appropriate for the duration of the remaining performance obligations.
- By using qualitative information if quantitative information is not needed for understanding the timing of revenue recognition.

Entities must provide information about assets recognized from the costs to obtain or fulfill a contract (covered extensively in the previous chapter), including:

- The closing balances by the main asset category (e.g., costs to obtain contracts, pre-contract costs, implementation costs).
- The amount of amortization and any impairment losses recognized in the reporting period.

Disclosures should include significant judgments and changes in judgments that affect the amount and timing of revenue from contracts with customers, including:

- Determining the transaction price and the amounts allocated to performance obligations.
- The timing of satisfaction of performance obligations.
- The methods used to recognize revenue for performance obligations satisfied over time (e.g., output methods or input methods).

These disclosures provide a comprehensive view of an entity's revenue

CHAPTER 8: CHANGES TO DISCLOSURES AND REPORTING

recognition practices and their impacts on the financial statements, enabling users to better understand the entity's performance and future revenue prospects.

Conclusion

This was a lot of information to digest all at once. A disclosure should be made that if an Individual Contributor has questions about any of the information presented here, and how it pertains to their work environment, they should consult with their manager. No accounting methods or practices changes should ever be made without management's approval. Present your managers with the problems that their organizations might face, but also with a solution. Hopefully, this guide will help you create a solution to a pitfall in your organization's financials. And it might be one of the few times you get visibility as G&A tends to be a thankless job.

If you liked the content of this book, please feel free to leave me a review. Feedback, even negative feedback, is always much appreciated. It will help me make the book better in the long run. My goal was to impart information to individual contributors that might be useful to them in their everyday positions in a language that is easy to understand. It's easy for Managers and others with CPA licenses to assume you have the same knowledge they do. They have that knowledge because they must continue their education to maintain their licenses, and they are under the assumption you are engaging in your professional development. For those of us without that requirement, keeping up can be a challenge. Hopefully, you can add understanding revenue from contracts with customers to your accounting utility belt.

Citations

Citations

Singh, A. (2019). *Welcoming the New Revenue Recognition Standard: Asc 606 Revenue from Contracts with Customers Second Edition*. Independently Published.

Incremental costs of obtaining a contract - RevenueHub. (n.d.). https://www.revenuehub.org/article/incremental-costs-obtaining-contract

https://www.eduyush.com/blogs/interview-questions/ifrs-interview-questions

Dissecting the New Revenue Recognition Guidance: Step 1 of the Five-Step Framework | Insights | KSM (Katz, Sapper & Miller). https://www.ksmcpa.com/insights/dissecting-the-new-revenue-recognition-guidance-step-1-of-the-five-step-framework/

Accounting for revenue – assessing the contract | John Hughes IFRS Blog. https://disclosurehub.org/2014/07/29/accounting-for-revenue-assessing-the-contract/

IFRS 15 Revenue From Contracts With Customers - Best Overview – Annual Reporting. https://annualreporting.info/ifrs-15-revenue-from-contracts-with-customers/

Comparison Chart of ICDS-IV, AS-9 & IndAS-115 - Income Tax - Ready Reckoner - Income Tax. https://www.taxmanagementindia.com/visitor/detail_manual.asp?ID=1907

https://www.dmcpas.com/article/revenue-recognition-accounting-for-variable-consideration/

https://www.sec.gov/Archives/edgar/data/1639920/000119312518092759/d494294df1a.htm

Changes to IFRS 15, part one | John Hughes IFRS Blog. https://disclosurehub.org/2016/04/24/changes-to-ifrs-15-part-one/

Revenue Recognition Disclosure Changes for Professional Services. https://www.mossadams.com/articles/2020/02/disclosure-updates-for-nonpublic-companies

DALKILIC, A. F. (2015). THE REAL STEP IN CONVERGENCE PROJECT: A PARADIGM SHIFT FROM REVENUE RECOGNITION TO REVENUE FROM CONTRACTS WITH CUSTOMERS. https://core.ac.uk/download/296912713.pdf

The ASC 606 transition for construction contractors: Disclosures - Baker Tilly. https://www.bakertilly.com/insights/the-asc-606-transition-for-construction-contractors-disclosures

Forshay, T. (2017). Exploring Revenue Recognition in the Local Community. https://core.ac.uk/download/233575729.pdf

IFRS 15, software, policies, judgements – Accounts examples. https://accountsexamples.com/ifrs-15-adopted-modified-retrospective-method-software-policies-judgements-customer-options-current-year-effects/

7.7 Allocation Considerations for Significant Financing Components | DART – Deloitte Accounting Research Tool. https://dart.deloitte.com/USDART/home/codification/revenue/asc606-10/roadmap-revenue-recognition/chapter-7-step-4-allocate-transaction/7-7-allocation-considerations-for-significant

Tafon, C. (2022). Implementation Critical Success Factors and Accounting Standard Codification Topic 606 Implementation Dynamics: A Correlational Study. https://core.ac.uk/download/516439715.pdf

A new system for recognizing revenue. https://www.journalofaccountancy.com/issues/2012/jan/20114806.html

How-toWhen should revenue be recognised are there exceptions to the general rule - Howto.org. https://howto.org/when-should-revenue-be-recognised-are-there-exceptions-to-the-general-rule-54160/

Munter, P. (2016). The New Revenue Recognition Standard: Implications for Healthcare Companies. Management Accounting Quarterly, 17(2), 30-39.

Loyd, B. (2018). Asc 606. California CPA, 87(5), 15-18.

(2019). Revenue recognition, January 1, 2019; Audit and Accounting Guide. https://core.ac.uk/download/568308598.pdf

Church, I. (2016). The Effects Of Accounting Standards Update 2014-09: Revenue From Contracts With Customers. https://core.ac.uk/download/345083003.pdf

(2019). Health Care Entities, September 1, 2019; Audit & Accounting Guide. https://core.ac.uk/download/568308582.pdf

Disclosures in ASC 606 - RevenueHub. https://www.revenuehub.org/article/disclosures

Levanti, D. A. (2020). APPLICABILITY OF IFRS 15 PRINCIPLES FOR THE BANKING INDUSTRY:AN ANALYSIS WITH REFERENCE TO THE CREDIT INSTITUTIONS IN ROMANIA. https://core.ac.uk/download/328006242.pdf

https://www.sec.gov/Archives/edgar/data/1639920/000119312518092759/d494294df1a.htm

Revenue Recognition A Comprehensive Overview of Criteria and Methods - ACCA COACH. https://accacoach.com/revenue-recognition-a-comprehensive-overview-of-criteria-and-methods/

IFRS 15, software, policies, judgements – Accounts examples. https://accountsexamples.com/ifrs-15-adopted-modified-retrospective-method-software-policies-judgements-customer-options-current-year-effects/

(2016). Revenue recognition : Accounting and auditing considerations, 2016/17; Alert. https://core.ac.uk/download/552596709.pdf

Also by Lost Pines Publishing

ASC 606 for Individual Contributors
Amber McGee, who writes under Lost Pines Publishing, is based in the greater Austin, Texas area, in the United States. She and her life partner have a blended family with three kids and four dogs. In addition to being a full-time accountant, she also enjoys working as the Board Treasurer for her teenagers' high school marching band, singing in choirs, and spending time with her partner and youngest son

www.ingramcontent.com/pod-product-compliance
Lightning Source LLC
Chambersburg PA
CBHW072003210526
45479CB00003B/1042